The Friendly World of ...

The Border Collie

By

Hubert O'Hearn

Published by Four Freedom Publishing: Non-Fiction Division

1st Edition March 17, 2016

Four Freedom Publishing
Ireland – US – Canada

www.fourfreedompublishing.wordpress.com

Table of Contents

Introduction

Well what is there to be said about Border Collies that hasn't been said before? I'm gambling that there's at least a few things out there, otherwise I've just wasted several moths of my life researching and writing this book and as for you; you've actually bought it, hook line and sinker. Perhaps that should be paw leash and collar, but let's just leave the whole sordid episode behind for now, shall we?

This is the second book in The Friendly World series of books about dogs. The whole reason for writing and publishing them is to celebrate the dogs themselves. If you've never owned a particular breed, we give you all the basic information you need. If you're a veteran owner, hopefully we give you some smiles, a few chuckles and a lot of entertainment.

At the back of this book you'll see some information about Rescue Dogs and also Border Collie Clubs. Please offer them your support.

Be seeing you

Hubert O'Hearn

March 14, 2016

A Few Words About Stella

Each day begins with a nose-to-nose meeting. I really don't know how, where or why Stella got the idea for the proper procedures in waking up a middle-aged writer so let's just say that Border Collies have minds that operate using the Scientific Method: develop a hypothesis, test it and if the results are favourable, adopt it into praxis. Regardless of all that, unless I am up very, very early, somewhere just before sunrise Stella will hop up onto my bed and with the stealth of a jewel thief she will creep up beside my head and then lay her nose in the gentlest imaginable fashion alongside mine. Thus I start each day looking at a black and white dog head in profile. She doesn't look at me, instead averting her eyes like a well-trained valet who hands over his employer's bathrobe without embarrassment. Once I make it clear that I am awake, she then smiles at me; oh yes, a sort of sideways grinning of the teeth that inevitably reminds me of the former Canadian Prime Minister Jean Chrétièn. Thus satisfied, Stella then hops off the bed and stands in the doorway until I am actually up and moving about. Should I tarry, muttering something about 'mmph fifteen more minutes' the process is repeated, with an additional placing of the paw on my chest as though to say, 'Look here old man, books aren't going to write themselves. Move your ass.' It beats the hell out of an alarm clock.

As I write this, Stella is curled up on my toes which is a fine place for a dog to rest on a chilly January morning in Ireland. I don't know as puppies ever consider their future goals and destinations in the same manner as human children, thus avoiding the likelihood of crushing disappointment, however even if she had I am quite sure that Stella never thought she would end up living in a semi-detached cottage in the Mayo countryside. The countryside in general though would have been a logical destination.

She was born six and a half years ago on a – let's be polite and call it ramshackle – farm outside the city of my birth, Thunder Bay, Ontario. My fiancée at the time, along with me and her two children had been in a running debate for a year regarding what kind of dog to get in order to complete our happy home. Kimberly's one insistence was that she wanted a dog that would snuggle up in bed. (I worked midnights, so I took no insult from that condition.) Amanda, the eldest, wanted something small and sleek – a fox terrier, or a boxer. I insisted on a dog that would pass the Frisbee Test, an ability to catch and return thrown objects. Bradley was playing video games at the time and so avoided the debate altogether.

Kimberly spotted the ad on Kijiji: **Border Collie X puppies. $50**. (Yes, our girl has a little bit of Labrador Retriever in her, or at least her grandmother did. No matter. As I have said many times and evidently am saying again, I urge anyone who is not planning on entering their dog in Breed shows to please get a mongrel for health reasons.) The price being right, Kimberly, Bradley and I drove out to the farm.

It was there that we saw the happiest little puppy that bounced out to greet us and placed warm little paws up on my pants in a heartwarming gesture asking to be picked up and hugged. That puppy was already spoken for. He was one of Stella's brothers. She who was to become Stella was laying in the shade under the bed of a pick-up truck, glaring out with the cold stare of a basilisk, a look she maintained for months. She wasn't angry or aggressive, merely unwilling to show any affection until it had been well and truly earned. Good enough. I've always been fond of women with a strong mind of their own so out came the wallet and into the car went the puppy.

Names are tricky things for both babies and dogs. You want to choose a strong name, no longer than two syllables, ideally with a hard consonant in it as at some point you're going to be finding yourself yelling it out in a field, forest or busy street. So on the drive back to our house, Kimberly and I held a short naming conference. Individually, we each had owned one dog. Her childhood dog was Twinkles, mine was a sadly short-lived cocker spaniel named Asta. As both of those were star-associated names, we chose Stella for star. That puts the lie to many, many – dear Lord *many* – people who have since thought she was named for Stella Artois. In fact, I've even stopped ordering that fine Belgian beer because it started to seem a trifle obsessive. Now I have to make sure I never name any future dog, goldfish or donkey Guinness. Of course, Stella's name also led to the hilarity when she would sneak out of the back yard and I would be trudging the streets calling 'Stella!' like a Method actor prepping for a community theatre production of A Streetchar Named Desire.

We now leap forward seven months or so. I had still been working midnights, five nights a week, so really much of Stella's puppy training and general family time was with Kimberly and the children and not me. Then, on a Sunday in February, my beautiful Kimberly had a brain aneurysm explode in her frontal lobe while we were standing in the kitchen. Her body lived, but her short-term memory did not. After weeks and months of hospitals and therapy, she had to move away to live with her parents, Amanda moved out on her own and Bradley returned to live with his father. From the front door of the house I watched the car with Kimberly in it drive away. I walked back into the living room and sat in the blue recliner placed where the Christmas tree used to stand, picked up Stella and placed her on my lap. 'Well, it's you and me now kid. I guess we better get to know one another.'

Two years later, we moved to Ireland. Why? Well really why not? There was nothing left to hold me to Canada and I had felt drawn to that little moss-covered island since the first time I was there at the age of ten. Thunder Bay was a permanent fog of loss and regret; a place where I used to do things I could no longer do, each day one more bad memory recalled. Writing had

kept my mind alive during what I later realized had
been a two year bout of Depression; writing and Stella.

I don't know if I would have survived all that without
her. You see, one of the side benefits of having a dog is
that if you have any sense of responsibility at all, you
have to keep moving, doing and living. She had to be
let out in the morning. She had to have her walkies. She
had to be fed. She had to have her cuddles. Every night
when I left to walk to work, I would hear her howl for
precisely ninety seconds – a habit that continues to this
day, any time i leave the house alone. I was needed.

Oh and I had a battle for her too. Stella has one bad
habit she has no control over. She sheds. And when I
say she sheds, I mean she creates fields of carpet fur.
With no exaggeration whatsoever, I have given the
floors a proper Hoovering in the morning and by the
time of afternoon tea I will be watching little
tumbleweeds of black fur rolling across the lone prairie
of my sitting room. While we were still in Thunder

9

Bay, because I was working that wretched midnight shift at a local hotel, my housekeeping tended to be put off until the weekend, save for washing the dishes. As such, her fur became welded to the carpets. Without a word of a lie, not one but two vacuum cleaners burnt out trying to rip the fur from the rug fibres. Kimberly's Dad – the house was in her parents' name – put his foot down and insisted I get rid of Stella. I don't blame him as I look back on it. No one knows how empty a life of Depression is except for the one living in it, and even then one only realizes the black void once the light has been re-discovered. However, I am so glad I still had the emotional strength to say, 'No. Don't you get it? She's all I have left.' We moved to a terrace for our last months there.

The move to Ireland made for quite a change in both our behaviours. For me, I had completely committed myself to a life as a writer, no excuses. Therefore every day was a work day, although as the late Christopher Hitchens commented near the end of his life, 'Writing is my recreation.' More importantly, I felt a sense of peace as soon as I stepped out of the plane in Dublin on the morning of 12/12/12 and that contentment has never left me.

Now, there will be those that will say that Stella was just picking up from my own mood, but *her* change was even more radical than mine. Truth be told, she had been a rather hyper dog all the time we lived in Thunder Bay, given to dashing about the house, demanding things be tossed or tugged, barking and worst of all she mouthed constantly – taking my fingers and thoughtfully chewing on them. The latter in particular annoyed pre-aneurysm Kimberly incredibly, as did Stella's refusal to cuddle. A lap was a bed of nails for her.

Formal training had accomplished little. Bradley and I had taken Stella to Puppy Kindergarten where she both fascinated and flummoxed the trainers. Her greatest desire was to herd the other dogs, regardless of size; granted that is a natural instinct among all Border

Collies. The learning tasks though were another matter.
Yes, she would sit, lie down, stay, come and so forth ...
to a point. Once she had obeyed each command two or
three times she was exactly like a bored five year old.
'Right. I have this one down. Do something else.' I kept
reminding myself that I admire independence.

Once we arrived in Ireland though, at the grand old
1850 stone gate house I had rented in Wicklow, she
became as mellow a dog as you would ever want to
know. Except for the rarest of occasions Stella never
barks in the house and, once she had explored the new
house she curled up on my lap. I have become quite
skilled at typing on a laptop balanced on a Border
Collie balanced on a laptop. She has also never
mouthed my fingers since. There was still one bad habit
left though.

In early March, she ran off. I had been outside chatting
with the landlord and when a car drove past the house
down our narrow country lane, Stella was off after it

like a shot. No amount of Stanley Kowalski yells would bring her back. I got in the car and drove down every road in the valley, went to the neighbours' homes, phoned the Garda Siochana (Ireland's police force) stations and there was no sign of her.

The worst of it is that early March is lambing season in Ireland. We were in farm country there in Wicklow and outside of the occasional bang of manure, it was absolutely beatific watching our neighbours the cows come strolling by the back fence each morning. However, the local farmers had a sad yet understandable policy of shooting stray dogs. Strays have been known to attack and kill lambs and, well, the farmers had to protect their livestock. I left the back door ajar for her every night, but no. Stella was gone for a week and I was quite sure she was gone, period.

Around five in the afternoon I had just started to fry up a small steak and some chips for my tea when my mobile rang. 'Have you lost a sheepdog?' In Ireland,

Border Collies are conventionally called sheepdogs. Needless to say, although I'll say it anyway, I was out the door and into the car like a shot. My house was about two miles from the village of Dunlavin and Stella was at a farm two miles further on the other side. She had lost perhaps three pounds, no more and was otherwise clean and healthy. Mind you, she always has had the habit of cleaning her fur like a cat. There was no major 'Oh thank God you've finally come!' greeting from her.Stella just hopped into the car – she always wanted the driver's seat – as though this was all perfectly natural. And yes, she ate my steak that night.

Since then, we have moved three more times. We spent nearly a year in Berwick-upon-Tweed in the north of England and close to the same in Bangor, Northern Ireland. Now thankfully we are well settled in Mayo ... in a house with a large garden, tall fences and a lockable gate! I rather doubt she would ever run away again, yet as the saying goes, fool me once shame on you, fool me twice shame on me.

Our adventures continue ... but right now my best friend wants her walkies.

It All Starts With Hemp:
The Origins of the Border Collie

I'm not quite sure where you stand on the subject of reincarnation, however given your fondness for our incredibly intelligent friend the Border Collie I'm willing to take a stab that you're at least open-minded enough to indulge in a little bit of fantasy. For instance, you know that pal of yours, that one who's always organizing the weekend pub crawls or tailgate parties? He was a Border Collie in a past life. Of course you remember your teacher back in Grade School, she with the death stare eyes, who while on patrol in the recess yard who from a hundred foot distance could freeze a group of boys about to get up to mischief. She was a Border Collie. And it is definitely fair speculation that your one Gran or Auntie who erects a force field to bring the whole family together for Thanksgiving, Christmas, or really any time she wants, *definite* Border Collie.

They gather, they organize, they watch. That's what Border Collies are, that's what they do. In a sense they are much like those people who come into your house and in either charming or annoying fashion instinctively adjust the pictures on your walls or the cutlery on your dining table. You know the sort I mean. God help you if you go to their house and remove a sofa cushion to the floor because it annoys your back. If sofa cushions were meant to be on floors, there would be floor cushions, so put that bloody thing back where you found it.

You may well already know that Border Collies were bred originally to herd livestock. Although we'll get back to that quite shortly, that herding instinct still presents itself even in the most domestic of circumstances. If you observe your Border Collie, you'll see that same desire to move and organize even if your home and backyard is miles away from the nearest sheep or cow. Let's say your dog has an assortment of toys. If on a warm summer's day you choose to leave the back door open for a little airing of the house, sit back and enjoy the gathering of the toys as they are carried outside one by one and presented to you. Yes, your dog wants to play (just forget about that book you were intending to read) but more importantly, those toys need their proper exercise.

So where did this obsessive-compulsive behaviour come from?

The general consensus among Smart People With Doctorates is that the first dog (*Canis familiaris*) was a descendant of an ancient wolf that was snuffling around Eurasia somewhere between 27,000-40,000 BC. The closest descendant of that lupine (a posh word for wolf) is the Gray Wolf found to this day in packs across Europe and North America.

Well that's one theory anyway. Another one, held by evolutionary biologist John Allman[i] places the dog and human relationship much further back, to 135,000BC. In fact, Allman speculates that it was through the cooperative hunting partnership of dogs and *homo sapiens* (that would be us) that gave the latter the upper hand over Neanderthals and *homo erectus*. In other words, if it wasn't for dogs we'd be Fred Flinstone.

Now one question that may have occurred to you is: Why didn't these ancient dogs just eat the people? Okay, maybe that question *hasn't* occurred to you, but there it is anyway. The answer is that dogs became scavengers because of cats. When the big cats such as the saber-toothed tiger showed up about 26 million years ago, with their claws and teeth they were much better kitted out for hunting large prey. The dogs decided, after several committee meetings and perhaps a lengthy referendum battle, that they would be much better off dining from the scraps left behind by the cats, supplemented by the odd mouse, rabbit or meandering small creature. And that my friend is why Scruffy bangs his empty bowl about the kitchen instead of making his own damn dinner. It's all the cat's fault.

Once the Human/Dog alliance began, hunting techniques led to herding. Our very distant ancestors had no weaponry to use other than clubs, variations on the pointed stick, rudimentary knives and a net. Even bows and arrows waited until 64 thousand years ago, modern times in relative terms; it took almost two million years to come up with those after the first rudimentary tools were made. Therefore, the game plan was for the dog to flush out game and the hunter huffing up behind would throw the pointed stick at it, or at close range heave the net over its head and set to clubbing and stabbing. This is why bird dogs such as retrievers or pointers learned to stand still, or those such as our Border Collies crouch with their heads down. Jumping up and barking a loud, 'Look! Game here! Look at the game! Loo -' were likely to get a spear to the ear. Here too, a passive-aggressive nature was the preferred psychology as the dog needed to move the game towards the hunter without having it take high-speed flight.

There's no real need to dwell on most of what else went on in canine development between then and the 1800s so we'll just flash through all that like the opening credits of The Big Bang Theory. Suffice it to say that farmers were always looking for further refinements to their four-legged farmhands.

If you have ever wondered where the border in Border Collie comes from, you'd be quite wrong if you speculated that it refers to a border within a pasture. Rather, it refers to the northeastern English county of Northumberland. When I say English I really should add the word lately to it as this region boundaried by the Pennine mountains, Hadrian's Wall and the North Sea was swapped or stolen back and forth between the Scots and English for centuries. Northumberland is referred to as the Border Lands in the UK and that is where the first Border Collie was born.

Incidentally, to be completist about all this, the second half of our friend's name – Collie – is less clear in origin. Depending on which etymologist (one who studies the origin of words) you consult, you may get a variety of answers. There are those who believe collie derives from the Gaelic or Irish word for useful, although as the modern translation for useful is úsáideach it's hard to find any resemblance at all there. More likely it derives from Colle which meant coal black in Middle English, as in Chaucer's Nun's Tale, 'Ran Colle our dogge' or Shakespeare's A Midsummer Night's Dream, 'Brief as the lightning in the collied night.' Onwards.

Much less problematic than its name is the origin of the actual Border Collie. All Border Collies trace their lineage back to one dog, whose name was one that the actor Woody Harrelson would surely applaud: Old Hemp. There has been much mucking about with inter-breeding over the centuries. The first sheepdogs, such as the Old English Sheepdog, were very good at watching over flocks, but weren't particularly fast when it came to herding them back to the stables. Thus hunting dogs and even greyhounds or whippets were added to the mix to bring a little speed to the breed.

It all came together nicely with Old Hemp's birth in 1893. The first formal dog trials had begun in Great Britain in 1873. The first one was held on October 9 of that year by one Richard John Lloyd Price and was held in Bala, Wales. The October date is of slight significance. In the Victorian era, the sórt of specialized farming we have today was essentially unheard of. By October, most of the crops in the UK had been harvested, whatever livestock there was to be sold as meat had been sold, and the new lambs or calves would not be emergent until after winter. The time then was perfect for farmers to take a bit of a holiday while the weather and light were both still halfway decent and do what men do best, hang about with one another, drink and argue about who is best at what.

Old Hemp was a champion amongst champions. He was bred by Adam Telfer, whose brother Walter had won the third competition. Adam put Old Hemp into herding competition at the bright young age of one, barely more than a puppy and he won. In fact, Old Hemp won every trial he entered throughout his eight year life. That may seem a rather short life, but he lived it with gusto, fathering over two hundred males and an untold number of bitches. He has left us with a fine legacy.

What made Old Hemp great? It seems that just as with many of us, he was the product of the influence of both his parents. His father Roy has been described as a pleasant and amenable dog, yet not one with much of a skill in herding sheep. No, it was up to Old Hemp's mother Meg to do the heavy work around the yard. This may or may not be apocryphal but the story is too good to let fall by the wayside; Meg was so intense with her staring down of sheep that she would go into a state of hypnosis or catatonia, stood stock still until snapped out of her trance. Old Hemp luckily enough got the best of both worlds, elsewise he would have been a dog that just sat around and grinned, staring unfocused into space. That would be another kind of Hemp entirely.

[1] http://www.animalpeoplenews.org/anp/2012/02/29/the-evolution-and-natural-history-of-dogs/

How to Choose a Border Collie

There's a reasonably good chance that you leapt to this chapter first. You want a dog and most specifically you've decided that you want a Border Collie. Now, rather than do the usual thing and type in *Good for you!* or an equally hearty *Let's get started!* I instead want to briefly do everything I possibly can to dissuade you.

Why?

I worked for a little over four years as a Financial Consultant before I gave up a life of crime to instead become an impoverished writer. We'll save that whole story for my forthcoming autobiography, *Whoever Gave You This Book Really Doesn't Like You Very Much*. Anyway, at the office where I worked we had a Mortgage Specialist by the name of Doug to whom I would take my clients if and when they told me they wanted to purchase a house. Doug quite sadly and tragically passed away a few years ago, however I fondly remember how he would start off the conversation, although the first time I heard it I was scared stiff. He would begin, 'What do you want to buy a house for? I've worked in Mortgages for seventeen years and I've never owned a house, always rented. If you own a house, you're stuck with it. It's a terrible investment, mortgage rates fluctuate, and if you get a job in another city, what do you do with the house?' On and on he would go, discussing taxes, cost of furniture, heating, repairs, I forget now what else he'd get into, until by the end of it the only clients who would ever sign on for a Mortgage were those who were absolutely determined to buy *that* house in *this* city. That was his point and I tell this story because his point is also my point.

A Border Collie, or any dog for that matter, comes into your world as a living being with complete innocence on his or her mind. She will do all she can understand to fit in, will adapt to your rules and family structure, but – and this is important – she has needs too. A dog is not a toy. You can't stick it in the closet when you're done playing with it, and you can't turn it off at night like your television. Your Border Collie will make mistakes. When he's sick, he may well not be able to control his bowels some night. And Border Collies shed. Oh my, how they shed.

Remember too why Border Collies exist in the first place – to guard and to herd. That means activity. A Border Collie does not exist as a muff dog, miniatures that were bred in order to be carried about as hand warmer in winter. If your living arrangements are an upstairs apartment or flat with no yard or garden, and if exercise is going to be a once in the morning and once at night single trudge around the block, please do not bet a Border Collie.

Their intelligence too is not always welcome. My Stella has learned in all three houses we have lived, in both Ireland and England, how to open the front door, the back door and how to unlatch the garden gates. Believe me, this was nothing I taught her. You really haven't lived until you're awoken at four in the morning by a knocking at your front door, you slouch down the stairs, turn on the porch light, open the door and there's your own dog, dripping wet from rain. That is how I learned to lock the damn doors even when I'm in the house.

That intelligence mixed with the Border Collie's intuitive knowledge and indeed desire to herd can make for a rather bossy companion. It is a great joy of mine watching Stella leap about, trying to fly so she can herd the birds (awwwww!). It was goddam scary when she was a puppy and leapt out onto the street so she could herd the cars (eeeeeek!). She will learn quickly what time is dinnertime and if you are a minute late – time changes in Spring and Autumn make for lively debates – prepare to meet the Doggy Death Stare followed by the Gavel Paw of Execution.

Just thought you should know those few things.

But there you are, determined anyway, just as I was and you want a dog of determined mind that stands about knee-high and can catch a Frisbee like Jerry Rice caught footballs. Although come to think of it, I never saw Jerry Rice catch a Joe Montana long bomb with his teeth. (Thinking) Ah yes of course, face-guards. I'm sure he could have done otherwise.

Iu allude to this elsewhere in this book, but certain points bear repeating. Do not feel obligated to seek out a 100% purebred Border Collie. I have noticed that among champion dogs the level of in-breeding has crept up to 13%, which is still south of the danger zone of a 25% in-breed which can lead to all manner of genetic issues, yet as it rises there are dangers ahead in the coming years. Besides which, the Border Collie itself is a fairly modern cocktail of breeding and so if a grandparent or great-grandparent is something else altogether, you may well end up with more dog, not less. After all, we're all mongrels ourselves unless we're members of the Russian nobility and look how that turned out.

If you're committed to getting a purebred, for breeding or show dog purposes it must be a purebred, then I suggest attending shows in your area and having a chat with the judges, trainers or the breeders themselves. A purebred will set you back some money. After a bit of research I discovered that the cost of a purebred puppy is somewhere between $500US to $5000.

Regardless, get the paperwork from the breeder before making your final decision and take it to a veterinarian. I go into what to look for in some detail in the chapter on Health so I won't repeat all that here. But please do your due diligence. You wouldn't buy a home without having a look in the basement first, so don't buy a dog without checking into its past.

There is one exception; and that is a Rescue Dog. It is highly unlikely that an abandoned or rescued dog in a shelter comes with breeding papers; it can happen if the dog has been abandoned because of the sudden death of the owner or similar calamity, yet those are rare exceptions. You may not know the age of the dog, it may have health issues and there may also be temperament issues because of abuse. However, if you have patience and love in your heart, you will have as loyal a companion animal as your heart could ever desire.

Returning to Border Collies, whether you are getting a puppy eight weeks old, or a mature adult, you have a tremendous variety to choose from in terms of colour, coat texture and even size. The varieties are listed specifically in the Border Collie FAQ chapter. Do be aware that a puppy's coat may vary from that of its parents and size can also be an outcome of food, just like people.

If you already have a dog or two in the house, and/or if you have children, when at all practical bring them along to the shelter or breeder to assist in choosing your new pet. Besides being a nice bonding exercise for all concerned, you don't want anyone in the house resenting the new arrival. This is especially true if your Border Collie (or a Rescue Dog that is Border Collie-ish) is past puppy age, say six months or older. Dogs have personalities and they vary very close to the same extremes as people. There are specific dogs that another specific dog simply doesn't like, and similarly not all dogs will like all children and vice versa. Particularly in the case of dog meeting dog, as mentioned in the chapter on Training, you are much better off introducing the two on a neutral territory, so neither one feels that their space is being invaded.

If you are one of those gentle souls who will take in a Rescue Dog, I am including some information in the Appendix as to who to contact for further information. In any event, if you need more advice, do feel free to contact me through the publisher. Enjoy!

The Most Intelligent Breed?

The general rule of thumb, or I suppose that rule of paw would be more appropriate, is that the Border Collie is the most intelligent of all dog breeds. After all, it can take a flock of sheep out to pasture in the morning, supervise all activities like a stern teacher on recess duty, then return everyone home in the evening before slouching back into the farmhouse and making the master a lovely gin fizz before dinner. Of course I'm kidding about the latter.

Illustration: courtesy @SusanAlisonArt

Or perhaps not.

We shall get back to the Border Collie's remarkable powers of perception shortly, however first we require a frame of reference. You or I get graded on school exams, have degrees on our walls or lost in the closet, or we do those damnable Stanford-Binet designed logic puzzles on Mensa tests in order to rank ourselves on a scale that begins with head lettuce and ends at God. How precisely is a dog's intelligence measured in the first place?

What are Intelligences?

Yes that was intentional and you're welcome. Mind you, dropping that clunky S on the end of Intelligence was actually done for a purpose beyond provoking a brief snort of chuckle. Intelligence really is more than one thing; it is a combination of things acting in unison. They in turn form a tidy triangular shape with each of the sides labeled as Learning (or Memory), Thinking, and Problem-Solving. The goal, the real test of intelligence, is to get all three working together in close unison in order to create positive results. In the absolute simplest form, we go through this process when we eat scrambled eggs in the morning, which as the famous British wit David Mitchell noted on television once is 'so simple a dish that it's name is its recipe.' There are your eggs placed before you and you take a taste whereupon you find them a bit bland. Your mind, your intelligence goes to work, and you almost (not quite) simultaneously have three thoughts:

a) Black pepper is the dried and crushed seeds of a vine found in India.

b) The application of Black pepper as found in a nearby cruet will add flavour to eggs.

c) Shake some pepper on the eggs.

Well now, that won't get you a call from the Nobel committee, however you have found a successful outcome to the issue of making your breakfast more enjoyable. What you know of pepper led to seeking it out and then applying it to the problem. Now on to the issue of salt.

No, let's leave the salt unshaken and get back to the matter of dogs. The issue of Learning or Memory can be tested easily enough insofar as it is the ability to acquire and retain knowledge of the distinct nature of this, that or the other. In other words, if you ask Scruffy to bring you your slippers and he trots back with a monkey wrench held in his jaws he's either just guessing or he's alerting you to a rather serious issue with the plumbing.

Every dog owner knows about their dog and object or verb recognition. Your dog undoubtedly knows that when you say 'car' that not only means the big metal thing in the driveway whose wheels it, ahem, washes each morning; it also means let's go for a ride. Sometimes of course you didn't mean or imply let's go for a ride which will cause confusion, argument and end with hurt feelings only solved with the gift of a cookie. I don't drive anymore, so this is your problem, not mine. Mind you, to this day whenever Stella sees an open car door she wants to hop in which has led to my easy familiarity with all my village neighbours.

Chaser, a Border Collie who is billed as 'The world's smartest dog' by a BBC program called Super Smart Animals, has memorized the names of 1,022 different toys and will retrieve any one of them by verbal command. Another Border Collie, this one named Rico, in a way trumped Chaser. Rico didn't need any stinking verbal command as this dog memorized the labels of over 200 products. In other words, Rico did not simply need to know the difference in appearance between a rubber football and a soft teddy; instead he knew the difference between a can of Campbell's tomato soup or Heinz and retained that knowledge for four weeks after just one exposure to the product. Whereas, how many times have you arrived home with tampons instead of dinner napkins? Yes, I thought so.

2. *Illustration: Chaser*

The issue of Thinking as it applies to intelligence is where the subject becomes vastly more interesting because thinking implies a knowledge of consequence; because I did that, this will happen. I am only stating the obvious (which as I'm sure you'll agree, is something I am quite good at) when I mention that this is where most of our own intelligence goes bashing into the rocks of the sea of confusion. Sure I'll stay for one more round, leads to sleeping through the alarm in the morning, but you didn't consider that at the time.

An intelligent dog is very *very* good at realizing consequences to a point where they will even use that most human of unfortunate strategies: deception. Oh yes, they know right from wrong but they'll try and get away with it anyway. When we lived in England, heaven knows I wasn't wealthy, but it had been a good week so I bought a delicious 2 kg or roughly 5 lb roast beef for Sunday. With careful cutting and the application of gravy, there would be meat enough for four days or so. All well and good. I had my dinner, sliced some off for Stella to put in her bowl and left the remainder to rest and cool on the kitchen counter. An hour or so later, when I went to wrap the rest and put it in the refrigerator, no roast. Severe admonishment and much finger-pointing followed, as did shunning. Then we came to the following afternoon, when I wondered what on earth Stella was hunting for under one of the couches in the sitting room. Out came the roast, intact from the night before, which she then toted back to the kitchen to eat away from my sight. Ah. Yes, dogs understand deception. I'm quite sure they learned it from humans, so don't blame the animal, blame the trainer.

The whole discussion of canine intelligence does go anthropomorphically absurd when we start to relate the intelligence of a dog to that of a human. I've done it several times already for the sake of humour (Whaddaya mean ya never noticed?) however some take the subject seriously. Dr Stanley Coren, who teaches Psychology at Canada's University of British Columbia is one of several academics who has used what I'll call the Dog Years formula to equate canine intelligence to that of people. You all know what Dog Years are – one year in the life of a dog equals seven in the life of a human, so a six year old dog is gliding into middle age and a twelve year old is a weary crock, etc. That formula is imperfect on many grounds, not least of which being that a three year old dog is at its peak intellectually and physically, and name me any human other than who, an Olympic diver?, who can say the same.

Dr Coren, in a July 2011 article written for Psychology Today, states that 'I came to the conclusion that dogs had the mental ability roughly equivalent to a human two-year-old. Further work led me to believe that the most intelligent dogs might have the mental abilities similar to a human two-and-a-half-year-old child.' There's a lot of leeway supplied by that modifier roughly and that is a good thing, for there is indeed a vastly different modality of human thinking against dog or other animal thinking.

Because of our capabilities with language, and here I am greatly in debt to the work in linguistics as researched and reported by Dr Noam Chomsky, whereby we can create an infinite number of creative thoughts that can be expressed in an infinite number of individually distinct sentences (we're never going to run out of new poems or song lyrics, so rest easy) humans are restless thinkers. A dog, even a Border Collie, may be restless from boredom and/or a need, yet it is not restless in thought itself.

Dogs are rather binary. If a dog like my Stella is hungry for a treat and I give her one, her need is met and she is pleased. Dogs don't dither over menus. Finickiness is not a counter-argument to that. Yes, Stella may be more excited if I tell her one night that her wet food is chicken based and she may just sigh with resignation if she is served chicken for three or four straight days, however she is not thinking about new ways of serving chicken. Even with play, a dog learns fetch or tug games, but she is not dreaming up and experimenting with new games. In contrast, observe any playroom of toddlers at a day care. They are forever stacking up or moving about toys, or each other, in different ways trying to find whatever formula it is that creates the most pleasurable experience; not just pleasurable, *most* pleasurable. There is a huge difference.

That digression was performed in order to assess canine intelligence in terms of the third category of Problem-Solving. A bright dog faced with a problem such as a sheep wandering off from the flock, will seek a solution. Do hard stares work? Does barking? Does chasing? Does giving it a good bump with the nose work? As soon as the problem is solved, the investigation stops.

The Rankings

Now I suppose this is what you've all been waiting for. What breeds of dogs are the smartest and which ... aren't. We refer again to the work of Dr Coren, this time in a July 2009 article for Psychology Today. His methodology was, I believe, sound. The classic tools of measuring the reactions of molecules, mollusks or men to a given stimulus just would not work with dogs. They cannot all be reared the same way in the same conditions by the same trainers. As well, given their enormous individuality, which specific dog will ever be considered its breed's standard in terms of intellectual capacity?

However, there is a group well-acquainted with breed standards and that is composed of the judges of Dog Obedience as registered with the American Kennel Club or the Canadian Kennel Club. They judge dogs of all breeds in both working or field trials as well as obedience. While an individual judge may have a positive or negative prejudice towards or against one breed or another, as Dr Coren interviewed in writing 199 judges the weight of their collective experience balanced any personal quirk. There were a total of 133 breeds which each had been observed and assessed by at least one hundred of the judges. This is about as safe an expert panel as one can get.

The results were even more uniform than Dr Coren expected, as 190 out of 199 chose the Border Collie in their individual top ten. On the opposite side of the scale, 121 placed the Afghan Hound in their individual bottom ten. Here are the lists:

Ten Smartest (ranked smartest to tenth-smartest)

1. Border Collie

2. Poodle

3. German Shepherd/Alsatian

4. Golden Retriever

5. Doberman Pinscher

6. Shetland Sheepdog

7. Labrador Retriever

8. Papillon

9. Rottweiler

10. Australian Cattle Dog

On the other hand, and here I will completely allow you to be like a good parent and huff, 'Well *my* dog is the exception!' here are the bottom ten.

<u>Ten Least-Smart (ranked smartest to least-smart)</u>

1. Basset Hound

2. Mastiff

3. Beagle

4. Pekingese

5. Bloodhound

6. Borzoi

7. Chow Chow

8. Bulldog

9. Basenji

10. Afghan Hound

It really all depends, according to my hypothesis, what the breed was created for. A pure hunting dog such as a Basset Hound or Bloodhound had one job – suss out game abd flush it. Herding dogs such as our Border Collie or German Shepherds had more complex tasks. And please please take note that any breed or mixed-breed can be trained to be a loving companion. (But my dog can whup your dog. Heh.)

Training Without Tears

Elsewhere in this book I've mentioned that absolutely everyone on Earth is a self-proclaimed expert on how to train a dog. As you're probably a resident of Earth (Vulcans are cat people) that includes you. 'By gar!' you say, for some reason speaking in pirate, 'I know how to train me dog! If I can raise me children, sure and I can train a young sea dog. Ha ha!' Well good for you. I admire your confidence. Oh well done you. But um, your children, eh? Might I enquire how many times over the past week have you mentally calculated the time remaining before those slack youths with their feet on the coffee table and their friends in your fridge head off to college, to marriage, or to a naval destroyer anchored permanently off the coast of Aden? Right then.

The first and most crucial point about training any dog,
not just a Border Collie, is that he or she has a
personality and brother is that going to be made clear to
you. Don't ever assume for one second that there is one
perfect technique for accomplishing anything in life and
if you think there is, well that's why psychotherapy is a
high growth industry in this country. Your dog has as
distinct a set of firm likes and dislikes as a fussy
gourmet in a French restaurant. Worse yet, your dog is
like that same diner who comes back to the same
restaurant every day to the same table and you're the
waiter. To successfully co-exist, you're going to have to
get to know one another and adapt accordingly. Oh and
incidentally, the tips he leaves behind are crap.
Literally.

So as we proceed with these various training
techniques, do bear in mind that you may have alter the
plan slightly in order to suit your and your dog's
lifestyle. For instance, if you're using food rewards, a
carrot medallion may be preferable to a slice of wiener.

Or, you may live in an apartment or lack a fenced-in yard. You'll figure it out. I believe in you.

Pee Pee Poo Poo

We are starting here because just as surely as night follows day, when you first began evaluating buying or adopting a dog, this was one of your first considerations. You took a long look at that hardwood flooring you laid down at $6 a square foot and for the first time in your life you found yourself asking the question, 'How badly *does* urine stain wood?'

The first step in house training your Border Collie begins with steps as in stepping outside. Oh sure, you'll have seen the ads for Puppy Mats, the canine equivalent of a cat's litter box, but frankly we take a dim view of such contraptions. In my opinion their use is just putting off until tomorrow (or next month) what can be accomplished today and there will be an inevitable amount of unwanted confusion and one-sided arguments when accidents occur. You get the dog trained – or so you think – to relieve himself outside, you remove the mat and then good old Mr Puddles decides it would be impolite to wake you at 4AM so he vents his spleen next to the basement door, just where he's been going for weeks now. In no way is he going to understand why in blazes you're pointing at your damp and naked foot in the morning and screaming his name accompanied by adjectives starting with the letter F.

No, it is ever so much easier to start the bathroom training immediately. Your dog is as territorial as a border guard. He or she wants to know what land is their land and what activities are allowed on it. So as soon as you have brought the puppy (this is all actually a bit easier with an adult dog, but the method is the same) home, take it immediately to whatever space you have designated as a chunk of lawn worth ruining. Walk your dog around the perimeter of that space, for however long it takes, if necessary setting down a bowl of water to prime the pump as it were. If the puppy starts to wander into Forbidden Places, just admonish him with a gentle yet firm 'No'.[1] When your dog does pee or poo, praise him with just as much love and joy as you did when your child brought home his first finger-painting home from school.

Now it becomes a series of repetitions. The moment mealtime is done, out you both go until the work is done. This may take up to half an hour, but suck it up buttercup and think of that hardwood flooring you're saving. Eventually you *may* (remember, all dogs are different) be able to keep a water bowl or even a food bowl constantly filled without fear of mishap, but initially at least only put water down when you will be in the room to observe your dog drinking, as the moment the slurping is done, out you go again.

Two other notes: House training is infinitely quicker if you already have an older dog or dogs. Those wily old veterans will show the younger ones the rules of the house like family butlers instructing new members of the kitchen staff. And, it must be said, accidents will happen. There will be more on this in the next section, but for now let's just say that when you do find that damp spot or steaming plop of canine by-product on the floor, just clean it up and get on with your day. If you catch your dog in the act, a louder and firmer 'No!' will have some effect, however if more than a few seconds have passed it is much too late to do anything about it. At best, if you are dealing with solid waste, scoop it up and take it along with your dog outside and drop it down at the appropriate place, then pointing at it with a triumphant motion.

Oh by the way, if you ever get so frustrated that you hit your dog because of your laziness in training, we know a guy named Random Dude Steve. Random Dude Steve will come to your house and hurt you. Badly. Never ever hit your dog.

Working on the Night Moves

Now that we're all happily remembering the hits of Bob Seger, you may be wondering what to do at night. There you are, fast asleep, enjoying that Special Dream you have, the one with the beach and sunsets, when you realize that it must be raining outside and the window's open. So you open your eyes, see the moon through the closed window and think, 'Dammit, that's not rain.'

Where and on what your dog sleeps is as personal a choice as what you yourself sleep in. It is possible to train your dog to not sleep or sit on the furniture – actually a good idea with Border Collies given that they can be extremely heavy shedders – if you are absolutely consistent in never *ever* letting it happen. This means no cuddles on the couch with you and no sitting on your lap unless you yourself are on the floor. But do be aware my friend that you are not home 24/7 and when you return to find a bit of fur on the Lazy-Boy, well, your dog just wanted to be nearer your scent.

Back to business. Unless your dog has a bladder infection or something similar, it will never soil its own nesting area. Therefore it can be advisable in the first month to coax your new dog into either a cage or good-sized pet carrier at night, or at least until the habit is established that sleepy-time does not equal pee pee-time. Make sure the container is large enough for the dog to stand up in and comfortably turn around in (yes, they really do turn three times before settling in), have a comfortable blanket or dog bed inside nd also include a bowl of water. Again: the dog or puppy will not pee in its own space. Just don't sleep in late!

Some dogs adapt quite quickly to this, while others will moan like a thousand keening widows. If the latter, your dog is ad and lonely and you will feel that you are a heartless bastard. You now have two choices: move the animal carrier or cage into your bedroom for several days, which can lead to the low comedy of hauling carriers back and forth in the middle of the night; or leave the carrier/cage door open. If you do the latter, remove the water bowl and be aware that an accident may occur. Ease the dog into being used to the contained space by coaxing him or her into it while you are in the room during daytime, sometimes clasping the door shut and sometimes not. This is going to be a trial and error process and there is no point in pretending otherwise. It is up to you and your dog's mutual and individual tolerance. Good luck.

Walkies!

Unless you want to look like a hilarious figure in an old James Thurber cartoon, being dragged down a street by a sixty-pound sprinter on the end of a leash, you're going to want to train your dog how to walk alongside you without tripping you, jumping up on pedestrians or dashing off at unusual cut-back angles like Barry Sanders in his prime.

There are those who swear by choke chains or spiked collars that will cause the dog discomfort (a polite word for pain) if he or she tugs at the leash. Yes, they swear by them. We swear at them. You do *not* need to cause pain to have an obedient dog on a leash.

Here is a delightful method: Get an extra-long leash, preferably 5 feet or so in length. Loop the clasp end through the handle and slide the loop around your waist, so leaving the clasp dangling somewhere around your ankles. Your children will now laugh at you and say you look silly. This can start an animated debate about their relative lack of fashions sense, but thankfully that will get cut off before you start muttering threats about changes to your Will as you have a dog to train. Attach your Border Collie's collar to the clasp end[2]. Now walk around the house normally, doing whatever you would normally do. Make coffee, get the mail, relax and read the paper, whatever. Ohhhh there will be much stumbling at first, but you both will rapidly learn to match steps with the smoothness and exquisite timing of a couple of Olympic ice dancers. If you keep this up, when you take your dog for a walk, you should be able to hold onto the leash loosely (but do wrap it once around your hand, just in case) with the confidence that you will be setting the pace.

Something to be aware of – your Border Collie may instinctively wish to leap at pedestrians, cars, bicycles, small animals or other dogs. If you see a hazard such as these oncoming, shift yourself between your dog and the problem and shorten up the leash in your hands by taking some of its length in your free hand. An oddity with dogs is that a loose dog looks with disdain at dogs on a leash. The *leashed* dog knows this and will want to put on a display of aggression. Just keep on walking.

You Know My Name

It may sound odd placing the issue of what to name your Border Collie in a chapter on Training, but look at it this way: Whatever command you give will be accompanied by your dog's name. Your dog will know his/her name and hearing it will draw imemdiate attention. Hence, 'Spot! Sit!' is more effective that just plain 'Sit!'

Now then, as to choosing a name, although a dog has proved capable of learning up to 1200 different different words and their meanings they are best at very short words with hard consonant sounds. Therefore, while you may want to choose one of those fancy-schmantzy dog show names like "Lord Fauntelroy of Higgins-Basketball Holmes" just know that when you call the posh little mutt you'd best call him by Fonzie, or better yet for the hard consonant, Basket. Also, imagine what it will be like if your dog slips out of the yard some evening and you have to hunt it down in the neighborhood. Yes, I speak from experience. Wandering the streets yelling 'Stella!' had people wondering if I was rehearsing for an audition as Stanley Kowalski.

The Four Key Commands

There is almost no end to the amount of commands, tricks or generally impressive things you can teach your Border Collie. However, it is neither or desire nor our purpose here to equip you for a future career as a halftime performer at NBA games or NFL halftime shows. Rather, let's get down to brass tacks.

There are four key commands that you must teach for your dog's safety and they are Sit, Stay, Come and Drop. You want your Border Collie to avoid trouble and avoid causing damage. Everything else is subsidiary to those needs.

All commands are some combination of verbal and visual signals. Dogs are more responsive to the visual, but particularly in the case of Come, yours may be at a distance or have its head turned away from you.

The first and easiest is Sit and this can be taught virtually from the first day you bring your puppy home. For the sake of this section, we will assume your new dog's name is Spot[3]. Stand in front of your dog and while using a simple hand motion (I suggest an upward raising of the back of your hand, as though you were throwing salt over your shoulder) say, 'Spot! Sit!' Spot will have not the slightest idea of what you are talking about. So, get down on your knees, repeat the command and with your free hand lightly clip Spot across the back of his knees, pressing down on his rump if necessary so he does in fact sit. You will now praise Spot like he's your boss at the annual staff picnic. You may if you wish give Spot a small food reward.

Stay is the natural successor to Sit. After Spot has mastered the Tao of Sit, while he is sitting there waiting for bits of sausage to appear from the sky, hold your hand up again, but this time palm forward[4] and say 'Spot! Stay!' then turn your back on him and walk away a few steps. Look back and ... there is Spot standing next to your toes. Ah. This is going well, now isn't it? Shake your head in the sorrowful manner your Dad did when he realized that his son would never cut it in the majors, go back to Sit, reward, then start the process again. The first time Spot doesn't follow you, move immediately to a joyful ...

'Spot! Come!' Slap your knees, clap your hands, wave him forward like you're working the flight deck on an aircraft carrier, do the hokey-pokey, just do *something* to urge Spot to romp his way over to you. You will then indulge in praise and (optional) treats. Thus you will feel puffed with pride, the Master of Your Dojo! and you will call the family together into the living room to observe your genius and Spot's received wisdom. Whereupon you will simply raise your hand in the Sit motion causing wise young Spot to – roll over and play dead. Pause. Your family will applaud with delight and you'll consider getting away with this mild deceit, but you won't. You won't. For God's sake man, you won't!!! Instead, just inform the family (who will instantly think of a thousand things they'd rather be doing, which may or may not include spackling that crack in the bathroom wall) that they should all observe the training session so they can do it too. They'll feel tricked – and they have been – but this gives you time to sneak out to the kitchen for a beer break. Rewards can cut both ways.

Leave It! is an important command for any time good ol' Spot picks up something he shouldn't. That may include shoes, books, letters, poo, kittens, socks, brassieres, food that's not his, toys, remote controls, ping pong paddles, bottles, carpentry tools, grocery bags and anything else that can break, cause harm or meow in anger. It is best to teach Leave It before Spot is toting around one of these forbidden objects as that may involve an emergency situation. What you do not want to do is find yourself reaching for the object and tugging it away. That is a game. Leave It should not be a game.

You can accomplish Leave It fairly simply. Hand over to Spot a toy then after he picks it up (you can even throw in a Pick It Up command if you are so moved) have a treat hidden in the palm of your hand. Point to a spot on the floor in front of your dog and say, 'Spot! Leave It.' Open your hand and reveal the treat. Trust us, he'll leave it. Repeat all this as often as necessary.

Yes there are many more commands that can be learned but master the above four first, moving out from the house and into the yard. When your Border Collie is 100% compliant, you can take your pet to parks, the beach or other outdoor areas (depending in local leash laws) and feel secure that he will be able to enjoy recreation times safely.

Random Training Concerns

__Barking and Moaning__

Border Collies are not overly verbal, but do recall that they like to be in charge and being in charge means alerting you to visitors or approaching danger; that can be in the form of evry passing car. If your dog take to excessive barking, there are a few techniques you can try. There are electronic bark collars that send a small yet tangible electric jolt when stimulated by a certain level of noise. They do work, but I really do not approve of causing pain and discomfort. It is more time-consuming, yet by sensible verdict better, to commence that training indoors. If your dog barks in the house and you want it to stop say firmly 'Spot! No Bark!' and repeat until he stops. It is likely that the sound of your loud voice alone will serve as adequate distraction. This is going to take some time and getting used to however. Do *not* however shout at the dog. If you do, in its mind you've started a competition. 'Yay! Let's play the barking game!' You don't want to play the barking game.

Meeting Other Dogs

As we have mentioned, dogs are territorial, little Robert Frosts with a firm belief in strong fences building strong neighbors. You simply will not know if your Border Collie will be a gracious and convivial host when friends bring their dogs over to your house until it happens. At worst, you may have an awful dog fight happening right in your hallway.

We suggest introducing dogs on neutral territory – a local dog park if your community has one, a public park, parking lot or even across the street if that is the best that can be accomplished. And do your due diligence once more. Ask your dog owning friend how their dog gets along with other dogs.

Dogs can be especially territorial when it comes to food. If everyone is staying for dinner, separate the dogs as much as possible and do not feed your friend's pooch with one of your Border Collie's bowls. There may not be a problem, but if there is a problem, it will be a big problem.

Children and Dogs

Frankly, this could be a book in itself. Your Border Collie with its cartoon face, long tail and alert ears looks just like a child's stuffed toy. Take a look at your child's stuffed toy collection and note the missing ears, eyes and tails. Exactly. Before, and let us emphasize this, *before* bringing your new dog home, tell your children in no uncertain terms to never ever pull on the dog's tail, ears or paws.

Your children or a friend's children may be nervous around dogs. Border Collies quite like children and his or her plopping down next to the kids can be quite frightening. Use the technique of keeping the leash wrapped around your waist so that your dog can be kept separate from the child and everyone feels secure. Let the nervous child at first toss a treat or two over to the dog from a safe distance, just to get comfortable. Nine times out of ten, within minutes the no longer nervous child will literally have your dog (drum roll please) eating out of their hand.

[1]One word commands are by far the best and keep them and the tone they are spokedn consistent.

[2]A quick note on collars. It should be just loose enough that you can comfortably slide two fingers between the collar and your dog's neck without your feeling any pinching.

[3]Yes, I thought just as hard about that as you assume I did.

[4]Do anything you want, frankly, but keep it simple and memorable. That's memorable as in for you, anyone else in the house, and of course Spot.

Fame!

Given their intelligence and trainability it is no wonder that the Border Collie has been a featured player in many films and television programs as well as books. Here are several of the best-known.

Shadow

Where is he from?

She actually. Shadow is a female border collie featured
in the Australian author John Flanagan's fantasy novel
The Sorcerer in the North (Random House 2006, US
edition 2008).

First appearance?

Will the Ranger finds Shadow at the side of the road,
injured by a spear.

Identifying features?

Her left eye is brown and her right eye is 'a manic blue.'
She is friendly and welcoming to people she feels are
kind, but has a good sense for danger.

Any notable achievements?

Yes, Storm finds the trail leading Will to Malcolm the
magician's home thus saving the day.

Huh?

Do you expect me to give away the whole story?

Yes.

Too bad. We writers have to stick together.

Black Bob

Who he?

Black Bob is a fictional Border Collie from Selkirk in the Scottish borders.

First appearance?

He first showed up in a short story printed in *The Dandy*, Britain's longest-running comic book, in issue 280 (November 25, 1944).

How popular was Black Bob?

Well let's see. After that first appearance in *The Dandy*, Black Bob starred in his own picture strip/comic strip that ran in The Weekly News from 1946-1967. His adventures with his owner, Andrew Glen, also ran in *The Dandy* until the retirement of the artist Jack Prout in 1968, although older strips were re-printed regularly. (Prout was given a Border Collie as a retirement gift.) There were also eight Black Bob books printed between 1950 and 1965.

Dog

Who he?

Dog was the star of Footrot Flats, a New Zealand comic strip written by Murray Ball between 1976 and 1994. Ball quit writing the strip when his own dog died. (We take a brief pause as we pour one out ...)

Are you quite alright?

Yes, I just needed a moment. The thought of a dog passing makes me quite sad. Right, I'm okay now. You have another question, yes?

Fame!

You were telling me about the comic strip.

Right right, yes I was. Well, besides the comic strip, Dog was also the star of forty book collections of Footrot Flats. But that's not all! There was also a stage musical, an animated feature film called *Footrot Flats: the Dog's ~~Tail~~ Tale*, and a Dog-themed amusiment park in New Zealand.

Wow! With all that, you'd have thought he's have a better name than, um, Dog?
He has a real name, given to him by Aunt Dolly, but despises it and has never allowed anyone to reveal it. For that matter, he has alter egos such as "The Scarlet Manuka" who attempts to 'liberate' cricket balls from being hit by Wal and his team, "Mitey Iron Paw", and "the Grey Ghost of The Forest", that appear from time to time.

So Dog is like Snoopy, then? (silence)

Did I say something wrong?

Snoopy was ... a Beagle.

Perhaps we should move on then?

Yes, I rather think that best.

Bingo

Fame!

Who was he?

Bingo was the star of the 1991 movie named – can you guess?

Bingo?

Exactly.

What's the movie about?

Bingo, a runaway circus dog saves the life of Chuckie , a young boy who is somewhat an outcast within his family. The two quickly become best friends - skateboarding, playing pinball, and doing math homework together. But Chuckie's parents discover the stowaway pooch and make no bones about the fact that Bingo will not accompany them on their cross-country move.

That all sounds quite tragic.

No, it's a comedy you idiot.

Oh.

No worries. Bingo, by the way, was a cross-breed although we shall assume that his intelligence and comic flair came from the Border Collie side of the family.

Mike (aka Matisse)

Who he?

Mike, also known as Matisse was the scene-stealing star of the hit 1986 film comedy *Down and Out in Beverly Hills*, playing opposite Nick Nolte and Bette Midler. Mike also played Matisse in the television adaptation of the film, which ran one season before disappearing into the foggy mists of trivia.

So was that it for Mike then?

Oh not at all! Granted, that was his only featured movie role, however Mike also starred in the TV movie *Spot Marks the X* as well as commercials for Toyota, Doublemint Gum, and Little Richard's video for "Great Gosh a' Mighty, It's a Matter of Time." Mike was also the last host of the Patsy Awards, which were the animal version of the Oscars.

Sammy Davis Jr. Jr.

Who he, and what's the deal with that name?

Sammy Davis Jr. Jr. (who for convenience sake we'll just refer to as Sammy from here) featured in the 2005 cult classic film *Everything is Illuminated*. Sammy was actually played by two different Border Collies named Mikki and Mouse.

I've never heard of this movie. What's it about?

It's a quirky thing, co-written and directed by Liev Schreiber, who you'll know from *Ray Donovan*, *RKO 281* (where he played Orson Welles) and *CSI* among many other credits. The story of *Everything is Illuminated* is, a young Jewish American man (played by Elijah Wood) endeavors to find the woman who saved his grandfather during World War II in a Ukrainian village, that was ultimately razed by the Nazis, with the help of an eccentric local. The first half of the movie is quite a bright comedy, then it grows progressively darker. You might well enjoy it.

Sadie

Who she?

Sadie plays a small yet vital role in 2013's supernatural horror film *The Conjuring*.

What does she do?

She refuses to enter a house.

She has to wee?

No you dolt! It's haunted and as you're proving, dogs are smarter than people.

Oh.

Moving on!

Fly

So is Fly a boy or a girl?

Ah, you're learning to ask the right questions. Fly is indeed a girl and she played the surrogate mother to Babe the pig, the titular character in the 1995 movie *Babe*.

Oh I remember that one!

Not surprised. *Babe* received a 97% approval rating, was nominated for seven Academy Awards (winning for Best Visual Effects), and pulled in over $250 million at the box office on its initial release.

Remind me of Fly's part.

Gladly. Babe, an orphaned piglet, is chosen for a "guess the weight" contest at a county fair. The winning farmer, Arthur Hoggett, brings him home and allows him to stay with a Fly, her mate Rex and their puppies, in the barn. Later on, Arthur sees Babe sort the hens, separating the brown from the white ones. Impressed, he takes him to the fields and allows him to try and herd the sheep. Encouraged by an elder ewe named Maa, the sheep cooperate, but Rex sees Babe's actions as an insult to sheepdogs and confronts Fly in a vicious fight for encouraging Babe. He injures her leg and accidentally bites Arthur's hand when he tries to intervene. Rex is then chained to the dog house, muzzled and sedated, leaving the sheep herding job to Babe.

Was Rex a Border Collie as well?

Of course! Here's a photo of both of them:

Their voices were provided by Miriam Margoyles (Fly) and Hugo Weaving (Rex). The two Border Collies were also in the sequel *Babe: Pig in the City* released in 1998, however they were fairly minor characters in that film. It did $80 million in box office receipts, or roughly a third of the original. I suspect a lack of Border Collie-ness as the cause.

Bandit

Who was Bandit?

Bandit, a male, was Laura Ingalls' second dog, both in real life and in her series of *Little House* books. According to the television version of *Little House on the Prairie*, originally he was a stray, and Charles noticed him trying to steal food. While on the way home to Walnut Grove, Bandit jumped on Charles' rig and became a member of the Ingalls family.

At first Laura disliked Bandit, she missed her old dog Jack and didn't want a new dog as replacement, Bandit liked Laura and would often try to play with her, but she would try to ignore him, Laura's anger boiled when she saw Bandit with Jack's old toy, Laura unleashed her anger on Bandit, but later she was sorry for her actions and Laura grew very close to Bandit and yet she never forgot her old dog Jack. In Season 9, Bandit went to Burr Oak, Iowa, with the Ingalls. Bandit was played by a most gentlemanly Border Collie named Jeffrey.

Famous Border Collie Owners:

James Dean

Tiger Woods:

Crown Princess Mary of Denmark:

Anna Paquin:

Jon Bon Jovi:

The Competitive Side

As we've already seen in our chapter on the history of Border Collies (*It Begins With Hemp* q.v.) it became a regular custom each autumn for the owners of these specialized herding dogs to get together, have a few pints and compare notes. Of course as any one of us familiar with the social bonding arrangements that emerge from those four little words 'a few pints' knows, frank and open differences of opinion will be expressed and there are only two ways of settling those. It's either flying fists or arrange a competition. As winning a side wager or two was seen as preferable to explaining to one's wife the absence of teeth upon one's return home, the first field competitions for Border Collies were arranged.

The first sheepdog trial was actually held in New Zealand in 1867. However, as there were no Border Collies present (given that they hadn't been invented yet) we'll just pretend that never happened and was just some colonial ballyhoo of which no further notice is required¹.

As far as the UK is concerned, trials began in the fields surrounding Bala, Wales on October 9, 1873. That event was organized by the journalist and author Richard John Lloyd Price. Amongst his books was the weightily titled *Rabbits for profit and rabbits for powder : a treatise upon the new industry of hutch rabbit farming in the open, and upon warrens specially intended for sporting purposes; with hints as to their construction, cost, and maintenance.* Incidentally, Price also founded the Welsh Whisky Distillery Company in 1887, having noticed that the Celts and Gaels to the north and west in Scotland and Ireland seemed to be making quite a splash with their own varieties of Amber Fist, so why not Wales? The venture did not go well and so Price off-loaded his distillery to a Bala businessman in 1900 who in turn liquidated the company ten years later. This liquidation can be seen from the perspective of today as a tragedy, for any man who adds liquid to whisky is no kind of a drinking man.

While his business may have gone to the dogs, Price's business *with* dogs was much more successful. That first competition near Bala attracted ten entries and some three hundred spectators. Its first winner was Tweed, a black and tan dog from Scotland described as having a foxy face and owned by a Mr James Thompson, whose own face was not described.

In a rather perfect bit of symmetry, the very existence of the competition led to the development of what would become its dominant breed, the Border Collie. As the trials in Bala led to off-shoots, a group of owners decided to take the show on the road to London in 1876, specifically to Alexandra Park; the actual park, not the similarly named Australian actress, as she's not that old. Without making too fine a point of it, the trial was a disaster. The majority of entrants were show dogs, not actual farm-trained working collies. To quote a report of the day, the show collies 'barked, yelped and lost control of many sheep.' The winner, almost by default, a common red coated working collie named Maddie, owned by John Thomas, a Welsh shepherd who probably was delighted at showing those London toffs what a real dog could do.

The trials continue in popularity to this day, drawing upwards of twenty-five thousand spectators plus television viewers across the UK and indeed around the world. So, what actually is involved in one? While there can be and are local or regional variations, we will go with the general description offered here:

The exact layout of the trial field can vary significantly. Most experienced handlers agree that there are certain elements that are important to ensure that the challenge to the dog and handler is a fair and complete test. These elements include:

- The dog must leave the handler and fetch sheep that are some distance away

- The dog must take control of the sheep and bring them to the handler

- It is against the dog's instinct to drive the sheep away from the handler so an *away drive* is a good test and should be included

- The dog and handler should be able to combine to move the sheep into a confined space, typically a pen but in some trials they are asked to load them onto a vehicle.

Other popular test elements that are often added include:

- The dog must separate the group into two groups in a controlled way in accordance with the instructions from the judge. This may involve some sheep being marked and the dog and handler working together to separate them from the rest or some variation of that. This is known as *shedding* and is almost always required to be done in a ring marked out on the ground.

- *Singling* is another test in which the dog and handler combine to separate one sheep from the group.

- Most trials include a *cross drive* where the dog is required to move the sheep in a controlled way in a straight line from one side of the field to the other in front of the handler but some distance away from them.

In addition there are various elements that may be added to increase the level of difficulty of a trial. One such example is the *double lift* where the dog is required to fetch one group of sheep, bring them to the handler, look back and find another group, somewhere else on the trial field some distance away. They must then leave the first group and do a second outrun to fetch the others and bring them to join the first group.

In most competitions the dog will be required to do the fetching and driving tests on their own. During these test elements the handler must remain at a stake positioned during the layout of the trial course. During the shedding, singling and penning the handler usually leaves the stake and works with the dog to achieve the task.

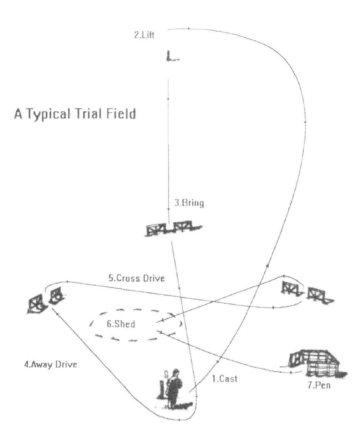

Other Sports

Just as surely as soccer led to rugby, rounders led to baseball, and golf led to divorce, field trials soon led to other forms of dog sport. The list is rather immense and not really worth re-printing here, however at last count there were some fifty-two distinct competitions ranging from Barn Hunting (wherein a dog must search out a vermin-scented can hidden within a barn) to Musical Canine Freestyle (effectively ballroom dancing for dogs) to Wheelchair Mushing for the disabled community.

There are three alternative competitions at which the Border Collie is both regularly entered and rises to conquer the challenges. They are:

Dog Agility: This one quite often shows up on late night television. A handler directs their dog through an obstacle course, competing for accuracy and speed.

Flyball: A relay race in which a dog jumps to fetch a ball and brings it back to the starting line as quickly as possible. When one dog gets back to the starting line after retrieving the ball, the next of the four dog team races away and the fastest team wins.

Frisbee or Disc Dog: The sport that launched a thousand football and basketball half-time shows. There are competitions for distance as well as Freestyle where the thrower and dog perform a routine consisting of various tricks, throws, and catches.

Just Showing Off

The Border Collie has not fared so well at traditional dog shows, where dogs are judged against a breed standard for body shape and temperament. No Border Collie has ever won Best in Show at either of the two biggest shows in the world, Crufts (UK) or Westminster (US). Westminster did add an Agility competition in 2014 and Border Collies won that the first two years it was held, before being edged by an Australian Sheepdog in 2016.

I have my suspicions as to the reason behind this lack of Best in Show winners. One obvious reason is that there are well over 100 breeds recognized by either or both of the American or British Kennel Clubs, so the odds are against any breed. Second, the Pastoral Group (that's the lovely UK term for what the AKC more prosaically calls Herding) as a whole has only won five out of a total of eighty Crufts championships. And third, well third deserves its own paragraph.

Because the Border Collie as a breed is fairly new (q.v.) the standard has not quite settled in yet. Just going by what I have seen with my own eyes, there are absolutely 100% pure Border Collies that are rough or soft-coated; brown, blue or alternately coloured eyes; black-and-white or tricoloured; and brindled or spotted as opposed to ruffed. The question of What then is a Border Collie?, may lack the poetic answers of What is this thing called love?, yet neither has yet achieved a definitive answer. It seems that recent Best of Breed winners at the big two shows are favouring soft-coated black-and-white dogs and that judgement will undoubtedly shuffle down the line to lesser or regional shows. Eventually I suspect that Border Collies will be sub-divided like various Spaniels into coat types. But really and in sum, Border Collies are beautiful dogs and marvelously adept at catching thrown objects. What more do you really want from a pet?

[1]Dear Kiwis – that was satire.

Health and the Border Collie

Border Collies are one of the longer-lived dog breeds, with an average life-span of 12 to 17 years. Some have even been known to live into their twenties. What has greatly assisted them in this regard is their relative newness as a breed, only achieving registry as a standard with the International Sheep Dog Society (ISDS) in 1946, the Kennel Club (UK) in 1976 and by the American Kennel Club in 1995. The advantage is that because other varieties of both gun/hunting and herding dogs were added to the mix, the bloodline of the present-day Border Collie has not become overly-refined and inbred. Border Collies have a Breed Coefficient (COI) of 4%. In simplest terms, this means there is only a 1 in 25 chance that the average Border Collie puppy will have inherited the identical characteristics of its parents, roughly the equal of breeding with a second cousin. A mother/son mating would produce a COI of 25%, first cousins 6.25%. A dog with a 6.25% COI *tends* to live four years longer on average than one with a COI of 25%.

Was that too much maths? Let's keep it simple then. Provided your puppy, if you are getting a purebred, comes from a mating of at least distant relatives then the strength of the breed will lead to a likelihood of a long time spent enjoying your dog. So there.

Now that being said, just as with any other breed of dog (or animal for that matter) there are certain diseases or physical defects that can show up with a certain minimal yet definable regularity. I can't urge you enough to have your puppy checked out by an independent veterinarian before purchase. Not all conditions will be observable in the first two months of life, but an ounce of prevention is still better than pounds of later vet bills dropping through the mail slot.

In fact, let's raise the stakes a bit higher – and here again we are assuming you are buying a purebred. According to the Kennel Club (UK) the breeder should be able to provide papers stating that both parents have been cleared for:

- Neuronal Ceroid lipofuscinosis (degeneration of the nervous system)

- CEA/CH Collie Eye Anomaly/Choroidal hypoplasia (CEA/CH)

- MDR1 (multi drug resistance)

- IGS (Imerslund-Grasbeck syndrome) (vitamin B12 is unable to be absorbed into the body – leads to loss of appetite, lethargy and malaise – long term treatment required)

- TNS Trapped Neutrophil Syndrome (immune deficiency causing recurrent bacterial infections)

- Canine cyclic neutropenia (Grey Collie syndrome) (stem cell disorder – very serious disease with multiple symptoms and death at an early age)

- Sensory neuropathy (SN) (severe neurological disease affecting young Border Collies – progressive loss of sensation in limbs due to the degeneration of sensory and motor nerve cells)

- Invermectin sensitivity

- Merle gene

If any of the information above is not available, do ask why.

Here are the major diseases or medical conditions found in Border Collies:

Idiopathic Epilepsy

Generally thought to be a trait carried over from the Shetland Sheepdog and Golden Retriever (two of the source breeds leading to the Border Collie descendant breed) Idiopathic Epilepsy is usually a genetic-based brain disorder that causes the dog to have sudden, uncontrolled, recurring physical attacks, which may or may not be accompanied by a loss of consciousness. Idiopathic epilepsy is often characterized by structural brain lesions and curiously is more likely seen in male dogs. If left untreated, the seizures may become more severe and frequent.

Symptoms and Types

Seizures are usually preceded by a short aura (or focal onset). The dog may appear frightened and dazed, or it may hide or conversely seek attention. Once a seizure begins, the dog will fall on its side, become stiff, chomp its jaw, salivate profusely, urinate, defecate, vocalize, and/or paddle with all four limbs. These seizure activities generally last between 30 and 90 seconds.

Seizures most often occur while the patient is resting or asleep, often at night or in early morning. In addition, most dogs recover by the time you bring the dog to the veterinarian for examination.

Generally, the younger the dog is, the more severe the epilepsy will be. As a rule, when onset is before age 2, the condition responds positively to medication. Behavior following the seizure, known as postictal behavior, include periods of confusion and disorientation, aimless wandering, compulsive behavior, blindness, pacing, increased thirst (polydipsia) and increased appetite (polyphagia). Recovery following the seizure may be immediate, or it may take up to 24 hours.

Dogs with established epilepsy can have cluster seizures at regular intervals of one to four weeks.

Hip or Elbow dysplasia

Border Collies are rather more prone than other active breeds of a similar size to developing hip dysplasia, an inherited condition that usually becomes apparent by the time the dog is two years old. Another condition that Border Collies are also sometimes prone to but rather less commonly than hip dysplasia is elbow dysplasia, and the two conditions will sometimes present concurrently. Border Collies that are known to suffer from hip or elbow dysplasia or that have an ancestral history of either condition should not be used for breeding.

Dysplasia is a genetic disease and has been claimed to be inherited from the dog's parents. Not only is hereditary, it is also exacerbated by many environmental factors, like weight and diet. It ranges in severity from dog to dog, dependent on age amongst other things, and can be very painful for a border collie. Visible indicators are your dog limping and having difficulty getting up from a lying position, and these signs generally appear when a dog is between the ages of four and nine months. The condition can be managed, including methods using different food supplements and other vitamins, as well as carefully monitored activity with reduced exposure to temperature extremes.

Collie eye anomaly

A third condition that makes up the trilogy of the most common Border Collie health problems is a condition called Collie eye anomaly, which is an inherited defect that can lead to blindness. How severe the condition is will vary from dog to dog, and there is no treatment for the condition. Caused by abnormal development of the eye, Collie eye anomaly does not generally significantly impair a dogs vision. There is a DNA test available now to ensure that breeders do not produce affected puppies.The disease is not progressive, and so the dog's level of vision will not worsen over time due to the condition.

Neuronal ceroid lipofuscinosis

Neuronal ceroid lipofuscinosis is a condition that is unique to Border Collies, but is currently only found within show dog lines and not working dog lines. It causes serious neurological impairment and a dramatically shortened lifespan; affected dogs rarely live past two years of age. The condition cannot be cured, but it is possible to DNA test for the presence of the gene within potential parent dogs, and so prevent breeding puppies that will inherit the condition or become carriers of the condition.

Trapped neutrophil syndrome

Trapped neutrophil syndrome (TNS) is a hereditary disease in Border Collies that leads to the body's bone marrow being unable to effectively release white blood cells into the blood stream. The effect is much like

AIDS in humans, although TNS is genetic andnot acquired. This disease causes a dramatically weakened immune system, and increases the dog's susceptibility to contracting and being unable to fight off infections and illnesses. Due to this, the condition usually proves fatal. Sadly, there is no cure or treatment available for trapped neutrophil syndrome, but DNA testing for the presence of the condition or the carrier gene can be performed.

The Merle Gene

Merle is a type of coat pattern caused by a specific gene, which causes a mottled colouration of the skin and coat and can also lead to odd-coloured eyes, with one of them usually being blue. Often, this coat pattern does not come accompanied with any health problems, but when two merle dogs are bred, leading to two copies of the merle gene being present in the subsequent puppies, this carries an elevated risk of both vision and hearing problems in the dogs. If you purchase or adopt a Merle Border Collie, please do not breed it to another Merle, or just avoid breeding in general.

Etc.

You may be having your doubts by now, but do trust, Border Collies are in fact one of the healthiest of all pure breeds. Your dog will have no health or welfare problems because of its conformation, a fancy term meaning breed standard. For instance, because of their breeding Great Danes are prone to colonic issues just as Basset Hounds are frequent victims of back pain.

Yet, we do have one more list for you to look at. There are a number of conditions that do not have screening tests. Instead, you must ask the breeder if there is any incidence of these in the present litter's parents or grandparents:

- Inflammatory bowel disease

- Idiopathic Epilepsy

- Patent ductus arteriosus (PDA) (failure of ductus arteriosus to close after birth, causing prolonged heart failure)

- Congenital portosystemic shunt (an abnormality of the blood circulatory system, resulting in blood from the heart by-passing the heart and entering the general circulation system)

- Osteochondrosis (shoulder and stifle) (painful abnormality of bone and cartilege)

- Border Collie Collapse (similar to Exercise Induced Collapse) episodes of disorientation and staggering, triggered by vigorous exercise, excitement or high environmental temperatures

- Cancer: testicular neoplasia; nasal carcinoma

- Squamous cell carcinoma (malignant skin tumour)

- Ciliary dyskinesia (abnormal cilia causing diseases of the respiratory tract)

- Hyperammonaemic encephalopathy secondary to selective cobalamin deficiency

- Haemophilia A (blood clotting disorder)

- Cutaneous lupus erythematosus (lesions on face and nose with loss of pigment and hair) (autoimmune disease)

Right then. Let's moved on to happier topics!

So What's for Dinner?

If your goal in life is to have a long and vicious series of arguments with otherwise placid souls who wouldn't care if you burnt down their house and toasted marshmallows over their family heirlooms, just bring up dog food. For indeed, there are two topics on which every man (for it is always men) are expert: How to Raise Your Kids, and How to Raise Your Dog. The divisions between commercial/homemade, dry/wet, table scraps/no table scraps make the Boston Red Sox v. The New York Yankees look like an ecumenical massed choir in comparison. So I think we both know that there are going to be arguments emerging from this chapter.

What I'm going to do is lay out the options as best we can and let you decide. There is no absolute, definitive science on any of this, particularly given that dogs have individual tastes and allergies just the same as people. Also do bear in mind that your Border Collie with its sensitive nose and refined sense of what is or isn't proper is well capable of detecting spoilage in what it is served. So if Mr Snuffles turns away from whatever is put in his dish some night, he may not be fussy. Rather, he may not be hungry at the moment (rare, but it's been known to happen) or he may not want to become sick. Maybe *you're* okay with a breakfast of cold pizza that has been left out on the counter over-night, but your dog may want nothing to do with the last servings from that unsealed forty-pound bag of kibble you kept next to the water heater in the basement. Dogs are not babies, however neither dogs or babies have any choice in the matter in terms of what they are fed. You have to do the thinking for them, so try and show some responsibility.

What We Do

Again, I wouldn't dream of insisting on my approach as the absolute or only way of taking care of your Border Collie's nutritional needs, but this is the technique that has kept my Stella fit and happy. She is fed twice a day with a cup of dry food/kibble in the morning and a 6 oz. serving of wet food with a high meat content in the evening. The occasional dog biscuit is perfectly fine, hard un-cooked beef bones for a treat are okay, and yes, playing catch with unbuttered and unsalted popcorn is fun for the whole family in limited quantities. Also, dare I say it, over the past six years there may have been one or two occasions where I have actually finished an entire sandwich, but I rather doubt it. Yes, I was the one who *Put My Foot Down!* in saying, 'Our dog will not be allowed to beg for food!' Then of course we actually got her and, um, carry on shall we?

You may now start screaming, *'That is all wrong!!!!'*

Fine. Now that you have that out of your system, we
can move along.

Dry Food

There is no small amount of controversy as to whether you should feed your dog dry food/kibble at all. After all, if we look back at your Border Collie's deep ancestral past, it's not like ancient wolves roamed the woods searching for bowls of bite-sized tasty snacks. That is the 'meat only' argument. On the other hand, if you have spent any time observing dogs at all, we are quite sure you have seen every dog start munching away at tall grass, the occasional flower and even bird seed from time to time. That is because your dog feels that from time to time it needs a little roughage in its diet, to sluice out the pipes if we can put it delicately. So unless, you want to train your dog into cutting the lawn for you[1], a little kibble makes a whole lot of sense.

That said, please do not choose your kibble based on whatever the most entertaining TV commercial happens to be at the time. This rule applies to both dry food and wet food, even though the evidence appears to the eye of a dog absolutely gorging himself on what must be the tastiest thing to ever *ever* be poured into a bowl. The old Tonight Show Starring Johnny Carson used to regularly feature live ads where Ed McMahon would give a dog a bowl of (**Snip!** - *Lawsuit Editor*) which the dog would vacuum down. One night a guest commented to Carson that the dogs really seemed to enjoy the food and the host responded that the poor things were starved for twenty-four hours to make sure they ate. Oh.

So what's in it?

Kibble is composed of a combination of meat, moisture and preservatives; most if not all brands also containing grains such as barley. The exact ratios vary wildly from brand to brand. Here are two examples, although we will not name the brands as we neither endorse nor condemn any specific product:

Brand A

- **Deboned Salmon, Menhaden Fish Meal (natural source of Omega 3 Fatty Acids), Chicken Meal, Potato Starch, Peas, Chicken Fat (preserved with Natural Mixed Tocopherols and Citric Acid), Potatoes, Tomato Pomace (natural source of Lycopene), Natural Chicken Flavor, Flaxseed (natural source of Omega 3 and 6 Fatty Acids), Alfalfa Meal, Whole Carrots, Whole Sweet Potatoes, Blueberries, Cranberries, Barley Grass, Dried Parsley, Dried Kelp, Taurine, Yucca Shidigera Extract, L-Carnitine, L-Lysine, Turmeric, Oil of Rosemary, Beta Carotene, Vitamin A Supplement, Thiamine Mononitrate (Vitamin B1), Riboflavin (Vitamin B2), Niacin (Vitamin B3), d-Calcium Pantothenate (Vitamin B5), Pyridoxine Hydrochloride (Vitamin B6), Biotin (Vitamin B7), Folic Acid (Vitamin B9), Vitamin B12 Supplement,**

Calcium Ascorbate (source of Vitamin C), Vitamin D3 Supplement, Vitamin E Supplement, Iron Amino Acid Chelate, Zinc Amino Acid Chelate, Manganese Amino Acid Chelate, Copper Amino Acid Chelate, Choline Chloride, Sodium Selenite, Calcium Iodate, Salt, Caramel, Potassium Chloride, Saccharomyces cerevisiae, Lactobacillus acidophilus, Bacillus subtilis, Enterococcus faecium.

Guaranteed Analysis
Crude Protein 34.0% min
Crude Fat 15.0% min
Crude Fiber 6.5% max
Moisture 10.0% max
Calcium 1.3% min
Phosphorus 0.9% min
Omega 3 Fatty Acids* 1.3% min
Omega 6 Fatty Acids* 3.0% min

Brand B

- Chicken By-Products Meal (Highest Quality), White Rice, Menhaden Fish Meal (Select Grade), Lard (the finest land-based source of the longest chain Omega 3 and Omega 6 fatty acids), Safflower Oil, Beef Fat, Dicalcium Phosphate, Beef Meat & Bone Meal, Potassium Chloride, Undefatted Beef Liver (Human Grade), Flaxseed Oil (Organic), Whey Protein Concentrate, Choline Choride, Natural Flavor, Menhaden Fish Oil, Ferrous Sulfate, d-Alpha Tocopheeryl Actate (Source of natural Viatmin E), Magnesium Oxide, Zinc Oxide, Ascorbic Acid (Vitamin C), Vitamin A Acetate, Taurine, Niacinamide, d-Calcium Pantothenate, Inositol, Citrus Bioflavanoid Complex, Ergocaciferol (Vitamin D3), Manganese Sulfate, Riboflavin, Potassium Iodide, Phytonadione (Vitamin K1), Thimaine Hydrochloride, Cupric Oxide, Chromium GTF, Sodium Selenite, Folic Acid,

Biotin, Cyanocobalamin Concentrate (Vitamin B12).

Guaranteed Analysis:
Crude Protein not less than 30%
Crude Fat not less than 28%
Crude fiber not more than 2.234%
Moisture not more than 5.98%
Linoleic Acid not less than 5%
Calcium min 2.4% max 2.6%
Phosphorus min 1.2% max 1.8%

What you will likely have noticed is the difference in Protein to Fat to grain or fiber balances (34%/15/6.5 in one, 30/28/2.25 in the other). So what is best for your dog? Even though your Border Collie is likely a highly active dog, you still don't want to risk it putting on excess weight; therefore our suggestion is to look for a food with at least a 2:1 ratio of protein to fat, and the more meat-derived protein the better. While it also makes sense to ask your veterinarian for advice, do be aware however that dog food companies target veterinary clinics and pay kickbacks on sales. It is perfectly within your rights to ask your vet, if s/he suggests a given brand, if s/he is being paid for that endorsement and on what medical grounds is that endorsement being given? You're not being rude, you're being wise; there's a difference.

Wet Food

One of the big advantages of wet food over dry/kibble is that the former has fewer chemical preservatives. Also, whereas kibble must have 50% carbohydrate content in order to be processed through the machinery, wet food has no such mechanical limitation.

That said, there are definitely things to avoid in choosing a wet food. Check the tin or other packaging for the names of certain additives. Carrageenan, for one, has been associated with intestinal ulceration, inflammatory bowel disease (IBD), and acid reflux. Besides carrageenan, it is possible that other thickening agents, such as carboxymethyl cellulose, polysorbate 60 and 80, guar gum, xanthan gum, and agar agar, may also contribute to digestive problems in sensitive dogs.

One other thing to be aware of in buying a wet food, is that wet means moist; it should not mean soaking! Yes, there will be upwards of 70% moisture in any packaged wet food, but numbers over 80% should really make you question why you are buying that brand, particularly if the remaining protein content is under 10%.

The Unfortunately Named BARF

The third school of thought regarding canine cuisine has the truly disgusting acronym of BARF, which stands for Biologically Appropriate Raw Food, or sometimes Bones And Raw Food. Although upon further thought, you have to admit it is a memorable name anyway, let alone terribly convenient if you want to kill a conversation with a bore: 'Good gosh Louise, I'm sorry but I have to run. It's nearly dinner time and I have to fill a bowl of barf for Scruffy.' Oh, that'll take care of that one nicely.

The theory behind BARF is essentially the same as the one behind human Paleo diets. In other words, what did ancient versions of these animals (or humans in the case of Paleo) eat, as that must be what the species was developed to absorb as preferred nourishment? As this book prefers its tugs of war fought over a length of rope rather than philosophy, we will leave that for you to agree or disagree with. At the very least though, BARF advocates have two strong arguments on their side: the whole issue of dodgy additives is avoided, and BARF can be cheaper than buying manufactured foods. As well, your processed food may say 'chicken' (or beef, lamb, etc.) but beaks, eyeballs and feet are just as much part of a chicken as thighs, breasts and drumsticks.

So what's in it?

A BARF diet is composed of the following:

Meat & Bones:

- Chicken backs/carcasses
- Chicken necks
- Chicken wings
- Chicken legs (thigh & drumsticks)
- Beef ribs
- Lamb (a little, as it is rich)
- Lamb ribs & laps

- Fish: Mackerel, Sardines, Sprats, etc. Canned fish (never in brine, so Spring Water, or Oil), or whole fish - head, tail, etc included. Salmon should be frozen first if it is fresh.

- Offal: Organ meat - heart, kidney, liver, tripe (also very rich)

If you are including vegetables:

<u>*Vegetables:*</u>

- Carrot

- Parsnip

- Green beans

- Squash

- Celery

- Cauliflower

- Spinach (small amount as it is rich)

- Kale (small amount as it is rich)

- Broccoli (small amount as it is rich)

As you have probably guessed by now, there are some controversies here. There are those who believe that bones are dangerous to dogs as they can splinter and damage the windpipe or gastro-intestinal system. The consensus however is that raw bones are perfectly safe, provided they are from the larger parts of the animal. A beef rib is good, but maybe avoid the smaller smaller, non-drumstick chicken bones, plus if you're afraid of fish bones why on earth would you feed them to your dog?

You may notice an absence of pork in the list above. That is because even commercially packaged pork may be contaminated with Trichinella spiralis. Trichinosis, also called trichinellosis, or trichiniasis, is a parasitic disease caused by eating raw or undercooked pork and wild game infected with the larvae of a species of roundworm Trichinella spiralis, commonly called the trichina worm. And lastly, those vegetables need to be boiled and pureed. Your poor dog just is not going to know what to do with a bowl of kale and cauliflower.

Things to Definitely Avoid!

Under absolutely no circumstances should you ever give your dog chocolate. It can kill them. That warning also applies to any product that contains cocoa. Other foods to avoid are:

- Alcohol

- Avocado

- Onions and Garlic

- Coffee, Tea, and Other Caffeine

- Grapes and Raisins

- Milk and Other Dairy Products (yes we know they love cheese, but no they can't digest it)

- Macadamia Nuts

- Candy and Gum

- Persimmons, Peaches and Plums (raw apples however are just fine, as are bananas, oranges and watermelon with the seeds removed)

- Raw eggs (although cooked are fine, including the shells)

- Salt (particularly in high amounts)

- Sugar (and you should lay off it too!)

- Yeast dough

- Human medicine (Really, just think for a minute would you?)

Jesse, Let's Cook!

Please excuse the Breaking Bad reference, but sometimes we can't resist. If you would like to make your own kibble, here is a recipe for you (courtesy and our thanks to Henrietta Morrison at thebark.com and her book *Dinner for Dogs* which I highly recommend):

All of the ingredients, except the turkey, are cooked in one pot. It takes about an hour to make and will keep for up to ten days. You can if you wish substitute ground chicken, duck, beef or lamb.

- 1 cup and 1 tablespoon (200 g) brown rice

- ½ cup (100 g) lentils

- 5 cups (1¼ liters) water

- 3 medium carrots (200 g), peeled and chopped

- 1 medium sweet potato (200 g), scrubbed and chopped

- 1 apple, peeled, cored and chopped, or ½ cup (100 g) unsweetened applesauce

- ¾ cup (100 g) steel-cut oats

- 1¼ tablespoons finely chopped fresh parsley

- 2 small sprigs fresh rosemary, finely chopped

- 2¼ cups (500 g) ground turkey, about 18 ounces

- ¼ cup (50 ml) olive, sunflower or canola oil, plus additional oil for greasing

Put the rice and lentils into a saucepan and cover with the water. Bring to a boil, then reduce the heat to medium and cook for 20 minutes.

Once the rice and lentils are cooked, add the chopped carrots, sweet potato and apple to the saucepan. Stir in the oats and chopped herbs and gently simmer for 20 minutes more. Add an extra cup of water if the mixture is too dry. Preheat the oven to 350°F/180°C.

Meanwhile, brown the ground turkey in a separate frying pan. You will need to keep stirring it while it is cooking to prevent it from sticking to the pan as it is very low in fat. It will take about 10 minutes to cook through.

Put half the cooked vegetable and grain mixture into a food processor with half the cooked turkey, add half the oil and pulse until the mixture resembles a thick purée.

Grease 2 cookie sheets and spread the mixture onto one of the sheets so that it is about ¼ inch (5 mm) thick. The mixture will spread slightly so leave a bit of room for this. It is important that the mixture is not too thick because it will prohibit the kibble from cooking through.

Repeat as above using the second cookie sheet and the remaining ingredients.

Place both cookie sheets into the preheated oven and bake for 45 minutes. Turn the kibble over so that it dries through, and cook for another 30 to 45 minutes. You should have what looks like two very large cookies. Make sure the kibble is completely cooked through, as any moist bits will get moldy after a couple of days. If it is not fully dried out, leave it in the oven for 20 minutes more.

Reduce the oven temperature to 325°F/160°C. Remove the "kibble cookies" from the oven, cool slightly and cut them into small pieces. Place the pieces back onto the cookie sheets and bake for an additional hour, or until the kibble is completely dried (but not burnt).

Remove the kibble from the oven and let cool completely. It should resemble pieces of broken pita bread. It will keep in the fridge for 10 days.

Per 4 ounces (100 g)

Calories: 365

Protein: 20%

Fat: 9%

Treats Please!

Just as you enjoy an occasional nosh and munch while watching the television, so too does your Border Collie. So what should you give or not give her ~~so you can~~

~~have some peace and quiet~~ for her own contentment
and health?

In the first place, your dog is going to want what you
have. This is why there's a great bundle of fur at your
feet or nuzzled beside you on the couch, with head
raised and as eager as a first baseman about to catch a
pop fly for the final out in the World Series. Your
Border Collie knows you well, and one of the things
she knows about you is that you tend to be a big human
cloud sending little snowfalls of crumbs to earth. I tend
to take my breakfast in the sitting room; since moving
to Ireland I have also become a big fan of the cooked
breakfast – rashers, eggs, toast, black pudding,
mushrooms and so forth. As I'm not all that smart, it
took me a good month to figure out that the wet spot on
the laminate floor next to my coffee table was *not* the
result of my spilling tea, it was Stella drooling. Ah.

Just as with your dog's primary food needs, do try and aim for natural solutions when it comes to snacks or rewards if you are training with food. There is a rule you should apply to human food that equally should be followed when it comes to dog treats or snacks: If it has a TV commercial, it's probably not good for you. However, I know that you will buy packaged dog biscuits because we're both ones for convenience. When you do, buy the most boring thing you can find. Look at the ingredients – if you see additives that remind you of entries on the periodical table of chemical elements, put the damn box back on the shelf. Avoid 'special flavours' or coloured treats as both are processed with possibly dodgy additives.

Things That are Good:

- bones

- pig's ears

- slices of apple, carrot or raw potato

- strips of poultry

- cubes or strips of sausage

Things To Avoid:

- Nuts

- Commercial 'chew strips'

- Crisps or chips (you'll drop enough anyway)

- Chocolate or berries

Jesse Let's Cook!

Yes, one more time. If you are a good-hearted soul and want to make your dog hearty, teeth-cleaning biscuits, here is a recipe drawn from Dani at Allrecipes.com:

Ingredients

- 1 1/2 cups whole wheat flour
- 1/2 cup all-purpose flour
- 1/2 cup cornmeal
- 1/2 cup rolled oats
- 1 1/2 cups water, or as needed
- 1/2 cup canola oil
- 2 eggs
- 3 tablespoons peanut butter
- 2 tablespoons vanilla extract

Directions

1. Preheat oven to 400 degrees F (200 degrees C). Grease cookie sheets.

2. Mix together whole-wheat flour, all-purpose flour, cornmeal and oats. Make a well in the center of the dry ingredients and gradually pour in water, oil, eggs, peanut butter and vanilla. Mix well.

3. On a flat surface use a rolling pin to roll out the dough. Cut the dough into dog biscuit shapes using a cookie cutter. Place the biscuits onto the prepared cookie sheet.

4. Bake the cookies for 20 minutes. After the biscuits have cooked 20 minutes turn off the oven off but let the biscuits remain inside the oven for another 20 minutes to harden.

[1]Don't! That was a joke dammit!

Border Collie FAQ

This is where we squeeze in all the odd facts, bits of trivia, general odds and sods that didn't float elegantly into a paragraph of one of the other sections. They are so presented here for your dining and dancing enjoyment.

Where did the first sheepdogs come from?

Remember that scene in *Monty Python's Life of Brian* when John Cleese screamed, 'What have the Romans ever done for us?' The answer, besides irrigation and roads should have included sheepdogs. Besides battling invading Tunisians and Visigoths, the Romans were quite good at agriculture including livestock. They developed and trained the first sheepdogs so that their owners could spend their days swanking and slacking in hot baths with Victor Mature and Hedy Lamarr[1].

When the Romans conquered the larger part of Albion aka Britain they brought sheep with them as well as their dogs. There was a slight problem though. Those dogs were rather large and used to a warm Mediterranean climate and so they didn't adapt particularly well to an island in the North Atlantic. So it was that when the Romans left Britain, the remaining dogs were adopted by the Celts, bred down into a smaller size and eventually became the sheepdogs and Border Collies we know and love.

What does my dog crouch and sort of slither? Does he have a sore back?

Well no, that rather odd stance and gait is part and parcel of the Border Collie's herding method. My suspicion is that this stance, along with the hard and fixed stare known as The Eye, were developed in order to be as intimidating as possible to sheep. The Border Collie wants to place himself at eye level.

What is the most unusual record held by a Border Collie?

I'd say that's probably Tropical Delights by Xavier Cugat and His Orchestra. It was only known by that title in the Dutch market, and elsewhere as Viva Cugat! Any dog that managed to glom his chops around one of these rarities can consider himself lucky.

Slightly more seriously, a talented border collie named Striker holds the record for Fastest Car Window Opened by a Dog. This fine fellow rolled down the non-electric car window in 11.34 seconds. Why anyone ever chose to make this a competition is beyond me, but then again someone actually thought of the rules of cricket too, so hey let's not argue.

How big will my dog get?

Males stand 19 to 22 inches tall and weigh 35 to 45 pounds. Females stand 18 to 21 inches and weigh 30 to 40 pounds.

What colours do Border Collies come in?

Why, so you can match him or her to your scarf? Just kidding. The Border Collie breed has two varieties of coat: rough and smooth. Both are double coats, with a coarser outer coat and soft undercoat. The rough variety is medium length with feathering on the legs, chest, and belly. The smooth variety is short all over, usually coarser in texture than the rough variety, and feathering is minimal.

His or her coat is most often black with a white blaze on the face, neck, feet, legs, and tail tip, with or without tan. However, he may be any bicolor, tricolor, merle, or solid color except white.

How often do they need brushing or bathing?

These are hardy dogs, quite self-reliant, so don't be surprised to see your Border Collie grooming him or herself much like a cat. Their weather-resistant double coat needs weekly brushing to keep coat oils well distributed, and to prevent matting in the rough variety. More frequent brushing during shedding season is a good idea to minimize hair shed around the house (they sheds seasonally, as in during all four). Bathe only as needed — about every four months or when he's really dirty or smells terrible. A good splash in a nearby river, pond or lake is on the whole much healthier.

[1]Or so legend has it.

Links

All across the world there are worthy dog shelters and rescue organizations. There is probably one very near your home and they all could use a helping hand.

While by no means comprehensive, here are some Rescue Animal specialists and Border Collie groups that I recommend:

USA:

Border Collie Society of America:
www.bordercolliesociety.com

Republic of Ireland:

Border Collie Rescue:

www.bordercollierescue.org

Dogs Trust Ireland:

www.dogstrust.ie

UK:

Border Collie Club of Great Britain:

www.bordercollieclub.com

Border Collie Trust of Great Britain:

www.bordercollietrustgb.org.uk

Romania:

Romania Animal Rescue

www.romaniaanimalrescue.org

Acknowledgements

I suppose really I should just thank every dog I've ever known and leave it at that; all the ones from Benji, who was a Basset Hound and walked me home from school, through to Stella who is lounging in the back garden as I write inside, on this first day of Spring.

Thank you to David Burns amd Claudia Cunningham for your enduring devition to the cause of animals, and the occasional itinerant Canadian. Thank you to Amanada Held and Bradley Gibson for helping me raise Stella (and do tell your Mom I love her dearly).

Thank you to my Manager, Pat Gregory and thank you to San Diego Book Review which keeps me supplied with great reading material.

And thank you Ireland. Without you, I'm homeless.